DISCUSSION PAPER 49

Endangered Democracy?

The Struggle over Secularism and its Implications
for Politics and Democracy in Nigeria

USMAN TAR and ABBA GANA SHETTIMA

NORDISKA AFRIKAINSTITUTET, UPPSALA 2010

Indexing terms

Politics
Religion
Secularism
State
Political power
Democracy
Islam
Christianity
Pluralism
Religious groups
Political conflicts
Nigeria

The opinions expressed in this volume are those of the authors
and do not necessarily reflect the views of Nordiska Afrikainstitutet.

Language checking: Peter Colenbrander
ISSN 1104-8417
ISBN 978-91-7106-666-4
© the authors and Nordiska Afrikainstitutet 2010
Grafisk Form Elin Olsson
Print on demand, Lightning Source UK Ltd.

Contents

Foreword

This Discussion Paper is based on an analysis of the relationship between religion and the crisis of democracy in post-military-rule Nigeria. It interrogates the oft-cited claims about the secular nature of the Nigerian state, as prescribed by the 1999 Nigerian Constitution, and points to the contradictions between the avowed claims of state secularity and the strong influence of religion on state-society relations and elite politics in particular.

The study also investigates the history, and conceptual context, of the role(s) of the religious factor in Nigerian politics, and its rather strong expression in post-authoritarian transitions as an instrument by which political elite factions seek relevance, legitimacy and access to power. The emergence of religious politics posed as "Islamic Northern" versus "Christian Southern" interests is both complex and misleading. As both authors argue, this formulation needs to be demystified, both in terms of the ways in which religion is manipulated in elite struggles over power and resources, in which advantage is taken of a "fractured and uneven citizenship" in various parts of the country, and the reality that some adherents of both religions subscribe to other forms of mystical traditional worship.

This study also shows how religious tensions and conflicts subvert and endanger post-1999 democratisation in Nigeria. The authors go beneath the rhetoric of elite secularity to explain the evolution of political Islam, represented in the adoption of Shari'a law in most states of Northern Nigeria (in which Christians are minorities), and the prominent position given to Pentecostal Christianity during the Obasanjo presidency. This perhaps marks a significant instrumentalisation of both religions at various levels by members of a government operating under a "secular" constitution. Apart from providing a critical analysis of the manipulation of religion by competing political elites, often leading to episodes of sectarian and communal violence in which ordinary people from both religious faiths lose property or even their lives, both authors draw attention to the hypocrisy of the same elites even in terms of the ways they instrumentalise religion for political and personal gain, with adverse consequences for social cohesion, peace, democracy and development.

However, the authors do not deny the existence of religious tensions in the country. Indeed, they accept and demonstrate the way religion has become embedded in Nigerian politics. They make the important point that rather than deny the obvious, focus should be directed at understanding the forces behind the use of religion as a modality of political mobilisation and conflict. Their main argument is that efforts should be directed at reducing the intrusive and destabilizing tendencies of "politicised religion" through the disengagement of religion from politics in a multiethnic society such as Nigeria, linking of citizenship rights with the deepening of democracy, promoting grassroots inter-faith post-conflict reconciliation, and the use of public enlightenment programmes to reduce tensions between the dominant religions in Nigeria.

This Discussion Paper should be of interest to scholars of religion, politics, conflict and peace in Africa, and is equally relevant to the needs of the policy community regarding support for democracy and development on the continent.

Cyril I. Obi, Senior Researcher
Leader of the Research Cluster on Conflict, Displacement and Transformation
The Nordic Africa Institute, Uppsala

Introduction

It is often said that African states have eluded development and modernity mainly because of the predominance of religion and "profane spirituality" in the public sphere. The recent visit to some African states by the Roman Catholic pontiff, Pope Benedict XVI, amid controversies over the Pope's mission and advocacy (for instance, on the use of condoms in preventing HIV/AIDs), buttresses the point that religion constitutes a key factor in the continent. There are claims that the Pope's visit was connected with the fledgling status of the continent, with its nearly 400 million Christian adherents, as the new hub of global Christianity: Africa is "the place where the future of the Christian faith is being redefined and determined" (Ilo, 2009). Another argument is that the Pope's visit is connected with the need to foster interfaith dialogue, particularly with adherents of other Abrahamic faiths and African indigenous religions (ibid.). Whatever the case, the fact remains that in Africa religion plays a pivotal role in the private and public spheres.

Religion has been cited as the "maker and/or breaker" of the African continent (Basedau and de Juan, 2008) and, in the context of democratic reform, religion seems to be an important factor in explaining why democracy and development have defied the continent. This study examines the contested construction of, and linkages between, religion, secularism and politics in Nigeria, and the implication of these connections for democracy. In doing so, the study recalls events following the restoration of democracy in 1999 after decades of military rule – as well as earlier antecedents in postcolonial Nigeria – in arguing that religion has been, and will continue to be, an anarchic reality embedded in the country's ambiguous capitalist (formation) and unstable political system. In this regard, we note that claims about the efficacy of secularism as a means of liberating the state and its public space from the shackles of sectarian politics is inherently problematic. This is so because secularism exists only in the faint imagination of Nigeria's self-centred political class and citizens, who are held hostage by all sorts of sectarian fragmentation. In a heterogeneous setting like Nigeria, where religion and others forms of socio-cultural and geopolitical divisions occupy a special place in power relations, religion cannot be simply wished away. Neither can secularism be entrenched in public life and executed in public policy. Thus, the domains of religion, secularism and politics are becoming increasingly intermingled in both overt and covert ways.

In most African states, the postcolonial era has not resulted in the much-anticipated development, much less democracy. In Nigeria, the postcolonial period has been dominated by highly contested, often short-lived, democratic experiments, sandwiched between prolonged periods of military rule. As this paper shows, sectarian politics seems to be central to the dearth of democracy in Nigeria. Events since 1999, particularly the rise of political Islam in the North and Christian/Pentecostal revivalism, have had a profound impact on the country's fledgling democracy and claims to secularism. Thus, taken-for-granted notions such as "the secular state" or "isolation of politics from religion" are rendered increasingly suspect, if not irrelevant, by emerging realities.

This emerges in bold relief when one considers Section 10 of the 1999 Nigerian Constitution, which states that "the Government of the Federation or a state shall not adopt any religion as state religion". This is an abstract provision that is far from reality: both the state and the governing class have always approved and supported religious narratives and symbols – such as divine revelations, mystical interpretation, mosques, churches, shrines, etc. – in advancing and promoting state policies. Indeed, some have argued that "this apparent affirmation of secularity is not the same thing as total rejection of (the validity of) religious practice" (Obadare, 2006:676). To be sure, the same section of the constitution also expresses the antithesis of secularism by affirming the resolve of the Nigerian people "to live in unity and harmony as one indissoluble sovereign entity under God". The key questions are, which God is the constitution referring to here? Whose God (with capital 'G')? Surely, writing God into a secular constitution not only constructs the state and citizens as religious but, perhaps more importantly, constitutes a recipe for conflict among adherents of conflicting belief systems, as well as those who believe in other spiritual and cosmic entities, or those who have no belief at all.

The study is divided into five parts. The second part of the paper examines the conceptual parameters of and linkages between religion, politics and secularism. The third provides an historical overview of politics, religion and secularism in postcolonial Nigeria. The fourth reviews recent developments to demonstrate the challenges to secularisation, in particular the rise of political Islam and Shari'a law in Northern Nigeria and the revivalism of Christian Pentecostalism as tools of political and religious expression and in the struggles for power. The final section contains concluding remarks and throws up issues for further debate.

Religion, Secularism and Politics – Conceptual Issues

The notion of separating religion from politics is a novel concept, particularly in Africa and the global South where there are clashes between tradition and modernity, and heterogeneity and pluralism have defined social relations. In the meantime, it is imperative to clarify the key concepts, religion and secularism, in terms of their conceptual and relational ambiguity in politics. Religion refers to any belief system in which adherents submit themselves to a particular supreme being – supernatural, material or cosmic – as a sacred independent entity with invincible capacity to supply a range of mundane and after-life satisfactions in return for unconditional obedience, devotion and loyalty. This definition applies to all faiths – for instance, African Traditional Religions (hereinafter ATRs, subsuming a plethora of age-hallowed beliefs), Buddhism, Christianity, Grail Movement, Islam, Sikhism and so on.

However, in this study, we emphasise the three "organised religions" that are prevalent in Nigeria – ATRs, Christianity and Islam. Organised religions are often characterised by a set of norms and values expressed through visual symbols (such as the cross or crescent); systems of worship (prayers, meditation, rituals); physical spaces for meditation (church, mosque, shrine); textual compendia (Bible, Qur'an); membership (Christian, Muslim, pagans) and a structured hierarchy, both horizontal and vertical. Though by no means exhaustive, these features serve as a *prima facie* basis of collective identity and action. In organised religion – and religious tendencies in general – there is an inevitable risk of power relations between different adherents.

Given that the religious space is inhabited by believers of unequal social and economic standing, religion (much like the market or state) remains instrumental in reproducing or questioning inequality. Perhaps more importantly, it stands as a structured sphere for the grooming of what Jeff Hayes terms a "theocratic class" (1996), defined as influential leaders/members of a particular faith/sect who have developed stakes in power and seek "to advance their personal and institutional position in relation to competitors" (Obadare, 2006:666). Suffice it to say that, while competition might be internal to a particular religion, emphasis here is on external competitors, those encountered in wider relations of power. The "theocratic class" is empowered by its capacity to inspire and, therefore, lead the governing class, the *de facto* wielders of national power and the appropriators of the societal means of coercion and of resources. As a parallel, default power base, the "theocratic class" derives its influence from its

> ... *power to preach, teach, dogmatise and lead congregations. They depend on perceptions of moral uprightness and justness, opposing themselves to the corruption of those in political power. They also rely on their charisma, their ability to arouse, inspire, and stimulate a crowd. (Falola, 1998:104)*

The foregoing discussion leads to the following points: (a) given that religions are essentially structured and characterised by vertical stratification, they have the capacity to either repro-duce or contest political power, both organisational and societal; (b) because religions are constructed as social and political formations within themselves, they serve as an incubation machine for the rise of a specific class, the "theocratic class".

In wider discourses, particularly in Africa, where most organised religions have been imported by external forces, religion is seen in diverse ways: initially, as a destructive "sectarian" force that characterises backward societies (see Greene, 2006); as an institution that will eventually fade away with the expansion and entrenchment of "modernisation"; as an institution with the potential to advance the frontiers of neoliberal democracy by speaking truth to power or engaging it (Haynes, 1997; 2004); and as an institution driven by "clear material reasons" (Love, 2006:622). There are concerns that more often than not religions appear to support anarchy, inequality and domination. This is not to dispute the impeccable role of some religious entities and leaders in supporting the cause of democracy, justice and the rule of law, as in Moi's Kenya or Nigeria in the 1980s and 1990s. Frantz Fanon's opinion, penned in the wider context of Africa, is worth considering here:

> *Religions split up people into different spiritual communities, all of them kept up and stiffened by colonialism and its instruments … sometimes American Pentecostalism transplants its anti-Catholic prejudices into African soil, and keeps up its tribal rivalries through religion. (Fanon, 1963:129)*

Similarly, Roy Love reinforces Fanon's position in the context of Islam and ATRs:

> *[the] expansion of Islam in Africa went hand in hand with hierarchical, and essentially class based, political structures headed by Caliphs, Sultans, and Emirs, or traditional chiefs and rulers. Many of the traditional religions of Africa also have special rituals and roles for chiefs, kings and their courts, or buttress councils of elders, almost invariably composed of senior males … In all such cases, religious belief is closely intertwined with the operation of a local political hegemony in such a way as to support a privileged male elite. (Love, 2006:625; our emphasis)*

The perceived negative effects of religion are the *raison d'être* for the emergence of "secularisation discourse", particularly in the context of nation-building and its attendant power relations in the developing world: these societies are perceived to be highly fragmented and susceptible to destructive religious tendencies. Nazik Yared defines secularism as

> *a refusal to believe that nature and history are governed by external, supernatural forces and a refusal to be guided by religion in political, social, educational, moral economic and other matters. (Yared, 2002:9)*

Inherent in Yared's definition as applied to the notion of the secular state is the fact that "religious beliefs and religious organisations have no constitutional presence, influence or affiliation – such that the state is able to guarantee freedom of thought, speech, peaceful civil activity to all citizens without prejudice" (Love, 2006:629). Thus secularisation is

> *a necessary result of the rise of the rational order that accompanies modernisation and political advancement … [Here] law replaces religion as a common organising principle of political life … [It is also] a social process involving the decline in membership, social influence, wealth and prestige of religious organisations, as well as a reduction in the religious fervour (religiosity) expressed by the membership of religious groups. (International IDEA, 2000:70)*

Others have advanced a more radical view of secularism. For instance, Connolly (2000) posits that

> *[s]ecularism is not merely the division between public and private realms that allows religious diversity to flourish in the latter. It can itself be a carrier of harsh exclusions. And it secretes a new definition of "religion" that conceals some of its most problematic practices from itself.*

Using Connolly's (2000) notion, it stands to reason that secularism is not a straightforward subject: while it may appear, at face value, to be liberating and neutral, in reality it is often quite problematic. For instance, it has proved relatively successful in homogeneous Western societies, where the societal evolution preceded, and gave rise to, the modern secular state governed by rule of law (see Tilly, 1975). In Europe, the Enlightenment era saw the emergence of the modern secular state governed by *laissez-faire* doctrine, rationalism and modern law. It also saw the gradual cultivation of the notion of "toleration", and of harmony between political and spiritual realms (Zagorin, 2003). This was the mould of political organisation which European colonialists sought to export to Africa, a heterogeneous setting where a plethora of cultural, political and religious outlooks exist in disharmony. Here, unlike Europe, "the sacred has refused to disappear or limit itself to the private realm, [and] it is effectively challenging the ideology that has sought to limit its operational space in many societies" (International IDEA, 2000:70).

In sum, it is argued that both religion and secularism are inherently problematic. The solution, perhaps, is to accept religion as an inevitable human construct and secularism as an imperfect solution. This framing allows scope for finding creative alternatives for governance. Below, we explore the religion-secularism conundrum in Nigeria's contemporary politics.

Religion, Secularism and Politics in Postcolonial Nigeria

There is no doubt about the need to understand the full ramifications of the connections between religion, secularism and politics in Nigeria, or the strategic urgency of secularism in that country. The problem lies in how religion is instrumentalised in politics, how secularism is rhetoricised and how politics is erratically constructed to serve the egoistical interests of the country's ruling and governing elites. Further, the contested nature of the state says a lot about the difficulties of institutionalising a secular state: capitalist structures (a key to secularism) remain blocked and distorted. It goes without saying that Nigeria is an ambiguous example of a capitalist formation, even by the standards of developing states. There is an emerging consensus that "the national bourgeoisie is relatively weak and divided by sectarian differences" (Tar, 2009:65). As a result, state power and structures are susceptible to prebendalism and neo-patrimonialism, defined as a "high degree of personalised rule, in which … the ruling and governing elites, are able to extract and redistribute patrimonial resources along regional, ethnic, religious and familial lines in order to consolidate political power and ensure regime survival" (Francis, 2006:81). Access to power involves both rational and irrational game-play, including, but not limited to, "the use and threat of violence, extortion, and outright plunder – not to mention traditional practices like witchcraft [and other religious rituals]" (Omeje, 2007:47; our insertion).

The Nigerian state has always been constructed as secular. This is a colonial legacy that has been carried forward to the current era, albeit only in rhetorical terms. Present claims of secularism are nothing but expressions of the imagination within official circles and undermined by the sectarian agenda of those in power. Exceptionally, there are those who genuinely advocate secularism. For instance, the Nigerian Humanist Movement (NHM) led by Leo Igwe has been principled and assertive in preaching the imperatives of secularism in Nigeria:

> In a multi-religious and multicultural society [like Nigeria], it is imperative that the state remains impartial for or against any religious or non-religious groups, or it loses its significance and value … it is only a secular state that is religiously and philosophically neutral that can guarantee the equal rights of every individual to freedom of rights, conscience and belief. (Igwe in Bujra, 2006:743)

Contrary to Igwe's admonition, the Nigerian state – more precisely, the governing class – has always been held captive by religiously motivated interests and forces. As Adogame aptly notes, Nigerian politics is characterised chiefly by "politicisation of religion and religionisation of politics" (2006:128). This reality is manifested in the nature of Nigeria's postcolonial state system, particularly the capture and control of state power by a self-centred, if divided, political class that strategically uses religion and politics to divide the people and consolidate and extend its control over resources and power in Nigeria's emerging capitalist formation. For instance, soon after Nigeria's independence in 1960, Sir Ahmadu Bello, the premier of Northern Nigeria, embarked on an "official" campaign to "Islamise" the North and eventually spread Islam to other regions. This drive generated, particularly among the Christians and adherents of ATRs, fear of looming religious extinction.

The assassination of Sir Ahmadu Bello in a coup led by a Christian Igbo officer in 1966 unleashed a spate of religious violence throughout the largely Islamic North and the rest of the country. In the 1970s, religion continued to be a pervasive and divisive political factor. For instance, the assassination of General Murtala Mohammed, a Muslim military head of state, by a Christian Northern ethnic minority officer in February 1976 led to violent reprisals against Christian minorities in the Middle Belt, the home region of the coup leaders, as well as a clamour for the establishment of a caliphate, along the lines of the Sokoto Caliphate that had ended with the British colonial occupation of Nigeria at the turn of the 20th century. The agitation for a caliphate culminated in the movement for Shari'a, which featured prominently, albeit without achieving complete success, in the constitutional conference initiated by General Obasanjo, General Mohammed's successor (1976-79).

In 1984, a coup led by General Buhari, which toppled the civilian government of Alhaji Shehu Shagari, soon gave rise to religious allegations from Christians, who claimed that the new military government was dominated by a "Muslim Militariat". General Buhari's Supreme Military Council (SMC) (1984-85) was criticised for being influenced by Islamic totalitarian principles, both in name and policy formulation. Following the 1985 counter-coup that overthrew Buhari, his successor General Babangida transformed the SMC into the Armed Forces Ruling Council (AFRC). He in turn was soon criticised by non-Muslims, who claimed that the change in name to AFRC was in compliance with Islamic doctrine that stated that only Allah is supreme. This fear was reinforced in January 1986, when the Babangida regime led Nigeria into the Organisation of Islamic Countries (OIC), established in 1969 to create unity among Muslims throughout the world, irrespective of their national and racial differences. Several non-Muslim members of the regime – particularly the vice-president, Commodore Ubitu Ukiwe and Minister of External Affairs Professor Bolaji Akinyemi – were eventually dropped, perhaps because of their perceived outspoken opposition to the new policy.

During the controversy surrounding Nigeria's membership of the OIC, Muslims pointed to some of the inherently Christian aspects of the Nigerian polity inherited from colonialism and never redressed in postcolonial Nigeria. In other words, they accused the Christian opposition of hypocrisy, of protesting only when they felt their privileges were being threatened. Such privileges included the adoption of Saturday and Sunday as days of rest, rather than Thursday and Friday or perhaps other neutral days; the adoption of the Euro-Christian Gregorian calendar rather than the Muslim *Hijra* calendar; and the scheduling of school and other national calendars around Christian festivals, such as Easter and Christmas, rather than, for example, the Muslim *Eid* holidays or *Ramadan*.

In the 1990s, Nigeria's military rulers appropriated religious rhetoric in more determined ways as a strategy of "divide and rule", with adverse effects on state secularism. This strategy was adopted against the backdrop of the military's bid to perpetuate power or, in the case of General Abacha, to resign from the military and contest as a civilian presidential candidate. The latter move was rejected by Nigeria's fledgling pro-democracy movement, which included many religious organisations such as the Christian Association of Nigeria (CAN) and the Catholic Secretariat. As Sylvester Odion-Akhaine notes, under Abacha's regime (1994-98),

> [m]ilitary administrators engaged with the Church to cast aspersion on the holy temple of God. It will be recalled that Army Colonel Ogar, who was military administrator of Kwara State under Abacha's junta, warned Catholic clerics "to stop paying lip service by annoying Christ" and also to stop quoting the bible to suit their purpose, due to their criticism of Abacha's self-transmutation scheme. (2006:760)

Suffice it to say that in targeting religious groups, military regimes often employ certain strategies. First, they call on the services of officials or regime loyalists in civil society who are adherents of that particular religion. For instance, in 1996 General Jeremiah Useni, the minister of the Federal Capital Territory, called on Christian leaders not to use God to attack political leaders and to "focus on leading their flocks on the path of righteousness, patriotism and obedience to constituted authorities" (*ibid.*).

Secondly, regimes are known to sponsor sermons in places of worship that laud the virtues of good followership and submission to leaders. By extension, they punish erring priests, imams and concierges of shrines, as exemplified by the public disgrace of Father Patrick Eyinla by the governor of Cross River State, Commodore Anthony Onyerugbulem, for not praying for the soul of the military dictator's son, Ibrahim Abacha, following his death in a plane crash in Wase, Plateau State. Finally, regimes use state-owned media to "preach" state policies. As Beckman (1982) argues, state media play a strategic role in mass ideological indoctrination, aimed at entrenching the powers of the ruling class. For instance, Abacha's desire to serve as a civilian president involved an elaborate campaign by the state's print and electronic media houses to extol the head of state as a gifted personality with supernatural powers.

Secularism in a Plural Society

Nigeria is a clear case of a heterogeneous plural society in which religious diversity coexists with other forms of diversity (such as cultural and linguistic). This reality has affected post-colonial nation-building. Nevertheless, there is relative consensus on the need for a neutral state, though how this can be achieved remains contested. While religion has remained problematic in Nigeria's "national question", it is interesting to note that secularism (its antithesis) is neither a religiously neutral concept nor is it a compromise among Christianity, Islam and ATRs (Kenny, 1996). As Mazrui (1986:16) contends, though the Nigerian state has been constructed as secular, "the concept of the secular state is itself Christian":

> And so the secular state in Nigeria is not a compromise between Islam and Christianity. The secular state itself is the triumph of one particular Christian tradition – a tradition which attempted to separate that which was due to Caesar from that which was due to God. This Christian legacy finally found its modern embodiment in the First Amendment of the Constitution of the United States, from which Nigeria has borrowed the principle of the secular state. (Mazrui, 1986:16)

This is indeed the most glaring irony in the conception of Nigeria as a secular state, which in principle means there is no state religion but in practice has obviously meant the triumph of a particular religious worldview to the detriment of others, especially the Islamic, which considers the separation of religion and politics as the very antithesis of all it stands for. In the Islamic worldview, "secularism is not only inadmissible but irrelevant" and the constitutional provision that "no state should adopt a state religion … in reality means nothing and solves nothing apart from the fact that it was borne out of a pathological fear and hatred of Islam" (Sulaiman 1987:38-9).

Thus the construction of the Nigerian state as secular is regarded as anathema by many and remains highly contested. Secularism in Nigeria is to all intents and purposes "a minority perspective in a country that explicitly regards itself as multi-religious" (Paden 2005:4). Similarly, on a BBC *Talking Point* programme, then President Olusegun Obasanjo was asked why he "let Sharia law exist in a secular state", to which he simply responded that "we are not a secular state – we are a multi-religious state. That is what we call ourselves in our constitution" (BBC, 2002).

Yet some still contend that a "secular space" does exist in the country. For instance, Nigeria's only Nobel Laureate, Wole Soyinka, is of the view that the secular space is a space "which is common to everyone; the space within which harmonious cohabitation is possible", and which must not be encroached on by any theocratic entity or component (*The NEWS*, 16 December 2002:25). It is, however, a matter of contention whether such a secular space exclusive of other social spaces exists at all, and if so, whether it is practicable in a multiethnic and multi-religious society encumbered with a neocolonial and underdeveloped economy.

Given the ambiguous manifestations of secularism in Nigeria, it is not surprising that the state – and therefore politics – has remained highly sectarian. Why is this so? Below we identify the key institutional and behavioural factors that underpin the illusory secularisation and the sectarian politics of Nigeria.

Constitutional Ambiguities

Nigerian constitutions have always enshrined secularism as a fundamental provision, though as we later note, this has been contested. In fact, secularism has not been explicit in the Nigerian constitution, though it is implied in the provision that no state in the federation should adopt a state religion. This situation has been compounded by the fact that almost all the constitutions have also contained controversial provisions, for instance in relation to freedom of religion and conscience, whereby Nigerians have unfettered freedom to indulge in all sorts of religious activities, particularly in political and public matters.

With reference to the 1999 Constitution, a number of ambiguous sections and clauses have undermined Nigeria's claims to secularism. "The overriding power of the Nigerian constitution versus the perception of Shari'a as 'God-given law' to be applied to Muslims – were (and still are) irreconcilable" (Harmeit-Sievers, 2007:144). Indeed, certain fundamental constitutional issues in Nigeria, such as the question of the supremacy of Shari'a law or the Nigerian constitution, are hardly ever resolved either by consensus or majority decision:

> In fact, Nigeria is a country full of such unresolved fundamental issues that are sometimes renegotiated, and sometimes forgotten – and one could argue that it is their very non-resolution that keeps the country together, even if it means that severe conflicts arise around them from time to time. Rather than driving conflicts to the limits on matters of principle, the various regional elites of Nigeria have usually resolved to just "put issues under the table" in order to ensure the survival of the country. The Shari'a issue is a clear case in point. (Harmeit-Sievers, 2007:145)

It should be noted, however, that such compromises on religious matters are reached or "put under the table" at the level of elites. In Nigeria's wider society, it appears that the real casualties of religiously motivated conflict are often the teeming masses.

Politicisation of Religion and Sectarian Fragmentation

Religion and other sectarian differences (such as ethnicity, sectionalism and culture) have been converted into a means to achieve and sustain power. Politicians openly espouse religious/sectarian sentiments in campaigning for public support. Indeed, a Nigerian historian has aptly observed that "no one can aspire to, or hold political office in Nigeria without pretending to be religious" (Toyin Falola, cited in Kukah, 1993:228.) The pretentions to religious piety among Nigerian politicians are akin to what Williams observed of the "tribalism" of the Nigerian bourgeoisie. This, he wrote (1980:40):

> ... is the outcome of its lack of control of the productive resources of the economy and hence of the competition among the bourgeoisie for favoured access to scarce resources, and the need to manipulate particularistic interests and sentiments among the poor to maintain the bourgeoisie's political domination.

The Nigerian political class exploits the powerful tools of ethnicity, religion and region to achieve its political ambitions, and to cover up problems arising from its failure to deliver development. For instance, following the series of ethno-religious conflicts in Plateau state, the then state governor, Joshua Dariye, characterised the whole conflict as a *jihad*, "'a grand design' and an *al-Qaeda* agenda to bring down Plateau state and bring down Nigeria". But it was obvious that the crisis in the state arose from the poverty-induced frustration experienced by ordinary Nigerians in the state and across the country. Such Nigerians daily witness the discrepancy between the deteriorating social and material conditions of the poor and the corruption and conspicuous consumption of the political class.

At the general level, public policies have to be religiously justified and key appointments to the armed forces, police, judiciary and various political offices have to be balanced in terms of ethnic, regional and religious composition, and it is not uncommon to hear shrill cries of marginalisation from different sectors in the country. Employment in federal, state and local government is required to reflect the "federal", "state" and "local" outlook in terms of geographic spread, ethnic and religious composition, etc. Moreover, the 1999 Constitution explicitly provides for the formation of a Federal Character Commission to ensure compliance with this delicate balancing act in employment at all levels of government. Similarly, institutions of learning, especially federal universities, polytechnics and colleges, are required to follow a quota system for admissions, which, in addition to merit, involves special admission quotas for applicants from the "catchment areas" of the institutions as well as from "educationally less-developed states", the latter admission requirements often being set below the merit quota, which is open to all applicants irrespective of state of origin.

Some state institutions also operate a regime of discriminatory, higher school fees for "non-indigenes" studying in such institutions of learning. For instance, at an internal displacement workshop following the 2001-02 ethno-religious conflict in Plateau state, some participants complained of the quota system operating in the state's schools that favours access for indigenes. This indigene-bias also operates in employment, even though so-called "settlers" pay taxes to state and local authorities and federal funds are allocated to the state and local governments partly on the basis of population, including the population of "settlers" (Global IDP, 2003:4). This discriminatory practice operates in almost all states of the federation. The Nigerian federation is thus highly contested, and the contours of the contest are often drawn along ethnic, regional and religious divides.

Bureaucratisation of Religious Institutions and Formalisation of Religion

Over the years, the Nigerian governing class has used state resources to construct religious edifices and symbols as a means of buying popular support and also to bureaucratise religions, in contradistinction to Emile Durkheim's notion of a puritanical state. The following are key examples: (a) the formation of Pilgrim Welfare Boards both at state and federal levels; (b) state sponsorship of Christian and Muslim "loyalists" on pilgrimages to Jerusalem and Mecca; (c) the construction of religious edifices in public places – mosques in state/federal establishments, including the presidential villa at Aso Rock, Abuja; (d) the "informal" allocation of religious quotas for elective and appointed posts, as if Nigeria's federal character has an unwritten clause encouraging the balancing of Nigeria's religious diversity in public offices; and (e) the declaration of Christian and Muslim spiritual events as "public" holidays.

Sunday Gabriel Ehindero, Nigeria's former Inspector-General of police who supervised the fraudulent 2007 general elections, was quoted as saying that when he was still in the post, he "brought God closer to the policemen. I established the chaplains in the Nigerian Police and they are there for everybody to see ..." (*Saturday Sun*, 9 February 2008, p.37). Apparently, in Nigeria's sectarian polity even the police force measures its achievements not in terms of its ability to control crime but by the number of its chaplains aimed at bringing the force "closer to God", whatever that means.

Leo Igwe points to the implications of the above trends: "Mixing of state and religion has caused a lot of trouble and confusion, anarchy, riots, destruction and bloodshed in the country" (in Bujra, 2006:742). Apparently, throughout Nigeria's chequered history, Igwe further notes, "the dominant religious groups – Islam and Christianity – have been locked in a fierce battle for the political control" of the country (ibid.). We return to Igwe's concerns in a later section.

Perverse Resonance of Contested Identities

Nigeria's federalism has always been contested, with religion a key factor. There are certain incorrect demographic impressions that pervade both policy and intellectual circles, with commensurate resonance in public opinion. A key example is the assumption that the North is "Islamic" and the South "Christian". To be sure, both regions have both Islamic and Christian inhabitants.

According to Usman and Abba (2000:14), the "North-South dichotomy" of Nigeria often emphasised in political circles is based on a false assumption about, and conception of Nigeria. The North-South dichotomy is rooted in the assumption that "the Federal of Republic Nigeria is an amalgam of two, distinct geographical, cultural, economic, social and political entities, namely, the North and the South". Usman and Abba argue that this assumption is false because "the amalgamation of 1914 did not amalgamate two distinct entities, standing apart from one another and having some cohesion on their own", and because the 1914 amalgamation was itself preceded by a series of amalgamations in both "Northern" and "Southern" Nigeria. In spite of this, sectarian conflicts manifest themselves along the religious-geographic spectrum. For instance, following the introduction of Shari'a law in the North, religiously motivated attacks on "Christian" communities in the North have resulted in reprisal attacks against Northern Muslims living in the South, and a number of Nigerians have become victims in this conflict. This reality has blurred the fact that members of both faiths reside in both regions.

Mystical Traditionalism and Power Politics

Somewhat related to the role of religion in national politics is mystical traditionalism, a phenomenon of which Nigeria's political class of both Christian and Muslim persuasion is aware (Omeje, 2006). This involves the reinvention of occult practices, cultism and superstitions in pursuit of personal wealth, influence and power. Such traditionalism exists not only in the shadows of mainstream religions, but also as a powerful tool in power struggles among both Christian and Muslim politicians.

Nothing illustrates the reinvention of cultism to advance political and economic goals better than the bizarre ritual killings in the forests of Anambra state in 2004 at the so-called Okija Shrine, at which police discovered the skulls and corpses of more than 50 people. It was revealed that those who patronised the dreaded shrine included the cream of society, including businessmen, civil servants and politicians. According to a priest at the shrine, "politicians come here to enact covenant and even two or more people entering into a business partnership in case one of them wants to cheat or double-cross the others ..." (*This Day*, 8 August 2004).

Similarly, nearly three decades ago, the report of the tribunal of inquiry into the Kano *Maitatsine* disturbances of the 1980s, in which over 4,000 people lost their lives, made the following poignant observation:

> *Evidence before the Tribunal indicated that some people benefited from the spiritual services of Muhammadu Marwa (Maitatsine). Looking at the number and position of people who patronised him, there was no doubt that Maitatsine considered himself immune from being touched or challenged by anybody, and this encouraged him to continue with his acts of terrorising people. (Report of Inquiry on Kano Disturbances, 1981:94)*

One fundamental issue arising from the Anambra killings and the *Maitatsine* episode is why and how Nigerian Christians and Muslims, who have supposedly professed a firm faith in God, turn their backs on their religions and worship at fetish shrines? Apparently, many who patronise the Okija shrines "in respect and fear" also profess to be Christians, just as many of those seeking spiritual powers from *Maitatsine*, the fringe and terrorist cult master, claimed allegiance to Islam (Shettima, 2004). When it comes to the struggle for power among both Christian and Muslim politicians, there seems to be no hard boundary between faith in the mainstream religions and adherence to bizarre cult practices. Thus, in Nigeria, religion in variegated forms and guises, served by the merchants and *marabouts* of a fraudulent spirituality, will continue to pervade politics, thereby rendering the nation's claim to secularity, however defined, totally suspect. Indeed, these developments have profound implications for Nigeria's secularity, as well as the place of religion in politics. Below, we provide empirical evidence from the Obasanjo era (1999-2007).

Religion, Secularism and Politics in Post-Military Nigeria: 1999 and Beyond

Nigeria's former president, General Olusegun Obasanjo, came to power in 1999 partly through his appeal to religious sentiments. Obasanjo's tenure and exit, too, were characterised by religious narratives and claims of power-sharing between Nigeria's Christian and Muslim "breeds" of the political class: "While Obasanjo's eight years as president symbolized an era of [Pentecostal] Christian control, even before he took office in 1999 political leaders began talking of alternating the presidency between the country's largely Christian south and predominately Muslim north" (Ruby and Shah, 2007). When Obasanjo was running for his second term in 2003, he said he was waiting for God to give him the mandate, and when his constitutionally sanctioned second term ended in 2007 and he was embroiled in the third term controversy, he said his God was a "God of continuity" and not that of "abandoned projects".

No wonder politics during Obasanjo's first term was plagued by religious division and bigotry.

> Under Obasanjo's presidency, a Pentecostal and evangelical revival in the south paralleled a rise of fundamental Islam in the north. An upsurge in violence in the Middle Belt reflects this tension between the north and south ... Religious organizations act as alternatives to the state and some argue that the weakness of government institutions, rather than ideological fervor, precipitated the religious revival. (Hanson, 2007:np)

A number of factors are pertinent in understanding Obasanjo's first term (1999-2003). First is the rise of political Islam, particularly in the aftermath of the adoption of Shari'a law by 12 Northern states of the federation. This phenomenon had commenced during Obasanjo's military rule (1976-79), but assumed dramatic dimensions during his "second coming" (1999-2007).

Second is the revival of Christian revivalism and Pentecostalism, which started in the 1980s but accelerated during Obasanjo's presidency. Third is the steady proliferation and entrenchment of "mystical re-traditionalisation" (Omeje, 2006), that is, the reinvention of occult practices, cultism and superstitions both in shadow of mainstream religions and as a tool in power struggles among politicians.

Shari'a Law and the Rise of Political Islam

Shari'a long antedates the Obasanjo era, having been in existence in most Muslim areas of precolonial and postcolonial Nigeria, though it came into the limelight in the controversial debates in Nigeria's Constituent Assembly of 1978 (Kenny, 1986). Christian and Muslim delegates differed over the proposal to establish a Shari'a court of appeal, which the former saw as an attempt to make Nigeria an Islamic state (Onaiyekan, 1987), while the latter argued that such institution was a fundamental right of Nigerian Muslims. A deadlock ensued resulting in the walk-out of Muslim delegates. Obasanjo, then a military head of state, intervened by declaring Shari'a a "no go area" in deliberations by the Constituent Assembly. As a compromise, the regime allowed for incorporation of what it perceived as a less-controversial-clause into the 1979 Constitution establishing the Shari'a Court of Appeal. The Shari'a debate, however, recurred in future constitutional debates, particularly those of 1989, 1995 and 1998.

On 27 October 1999, barely four months into Obasanjo's first term as democratic president, Governor Ahmed Sani Yerima of Zamfara state inaugurated the adoption of the Shari'a legal system in the state. For the first time in Nigeria's history, Shari'a had been extended from personal into criminal law. Eleven more Northern states followed Zamfara's example and joined the "Shari'a Club". However, not all Northern states adopted Sharia. Three patterns are discernible: (a) 11 states adopted Shari'a partly because of public pressure, particularly from the Northern "Talibans", to follow the "brave path" taken by Zamfara; (b) in states such as Plateau, with non-Muslims at the helm of affairs, it was practically impossible to adopt Shari'a; and (c) in other states, such as Nasarawa, the government, although headed by a Muslim governor (Abdullahi Adamu in Nasarawa), refused to yield to pressure for Shari'a on in order to avoid worsening the already tense Christian-Muslim relations in the state.

The Shari'a movement did not go uncontested. For instance, in Kaduna State, the state house of assembly's attempt to pass a Shari'a bill into law led to series of demonstrations by non-Muslims. On 21 February 2000, one such protest led to violent conflict, with many lives being lost and religious buildings and personal property destroyed. As an independent inquiry reported:

> *The scale of massacres and destruction was very high and thousands of people were reported to have been slaughtered like rams. People were said to have organised the killing of their neighbours simply because they belonged to a different religious order. This phenomenon led to a major restructuring of the town [Kaduna] with people congregating in areas where their religious faith had a majority of inhabitants. (International IDEA, 2000:75)*

Kaduna is now described as "Beirutised", that is, balkanised into Christian and Muslim areas. While Kaduna exemplifies an extreme religious and ethnic divide, similar settlement patterns abound throughout the country.

Throughout the North and Nigeria at large, the Shari'a debacle fostered acute insecurity among various groups, particularly those who "feared that the new legal regime would affect them adversely, despite claims to the contrary by Muslim supporters. Indeed many voices on both sides called for the partition of Nigeria rather than the adoption/abandonment of the Shari'a legal system" (International IDEA, *ibid.*). Shari'a-induced conflicts gave rise to a plethora of conflict zones, including reprisal killings of Muslims of suspected Northern origin and the burning of mosques in Aba and Owerri by angry Christian Igbo youths, who accused Northerners of killing and maiming their kith and kin in the North.

The federal government was forced to intervene, presumably to assert its secular authority, but with disastrous consequences. President Obasanjo called an emergency meeting of the National Council of State, comprising himself, state governors and former heads of state. It is relevant to note that the Council was dominated by Muslims since Obasanjo was the only Christian among the heads of state and the majority of state governors were Muslim. Nevertheless, at the end of the meeting it was announced that Shari'a legal systems would be suspended in favour of the Penal Code. However, two former heads of state and members of the Council – Alhaji Shehu Shagari and General Muhammadu Buhari – denied that any such decision had been reached, pointing out instead that Muslims were not prepared to forgo Shari'a. To be sure, Shari'a-practising states continued to implement all aspects of Shari'a law, leading to further riots and debate over such matters as amputation, public flogging of criminals, inheritance, etc.

The Obasanjo era witnessed a new phase in the Shari'a phenomenon, in particular the mass adoption of this legal system by majority of Northern states, as well as the rise of what some regard as an "Islamic fundamentalist" constituency. Most political commentators, particularly in Southern Nigeria, interpreted the 1999 introduction of Shari'a in Zamfara and its subsequent adoption in 11 other states as a deliberate ploy to scuttle the Obasanjo presidency. According to *Tell* magazine, for example, certain powerful Northern interests who thought Obasanjo was going to be "their lackey'" suddenly found that he was "independent minded", and therefore decided to use Shari'a to plunge the country into confusion. The magazine's headline reads: *Sharia Time Bomb: The New Plot Against Obasanjo* (*Tell*, No. 46, 15 November 1999:12-24).

However, it appears that in the period 1999-2003 Obasanjo also manipulated religion to serve his political purposes. For instance, he built and commissioned a chapel in the presidential villa and employed the services of a resident (Baptist) chaplain at the new Aso Rock Villa Chapel. This move paralleled the construction of a mosque by an earlier military regime. Members of Obasanjo's cabinet and his "Pentecostal constituency" used this circumstance to claim that God was in the process of cleansing the seat of the head of state of the residue of "satanic tenants" and "jihadists", thereby castigating its previous Muslim occupants.

According to an editorial in the *Daily Trust*, the leading newspaper in the North and one of the most influential nationwide, no government in recent times has cynically manipulated religion as the Obasanjo administration. "It has become a derigueur every week on public television, for the viewers to be inflicted with the spectacle of a live telecast of the Sunday service at the villa chapel, an event which is unprecedented in our national life, ostensibly to showcase how passionately religious our President is" (*Daily Trust* Editorial, 3 June 2003). More generally, the editorial made an important observation on the manipulation of religion in Nigerian politics:

> *A notable practice of the different Heads of State, Governors, Ministers and other top government functionaries, who have ruled and in many cases, ruined our country, is how much effort these people have expended to underline their religious bona fides, through outward displays of religious zeal and an unrivalled ability to manipulate the religious passion of the Nigerian people ... the Nigerian ruling class makes very loud claims to religious piety ... It is part of our national legacy, that as the crises of the neo-colonial state deepened, with the people finding escapist routes in fervent fundamentalist religious confessions, so has the proclivity of the ruling circles to exploit and manipulate religion reached new heights. (ibid.)*

It is reasonable to argue that the political class's claim to "religious piety" is symptomatic of the absence of secularism as an overarching state policy, as well as of the continued use of religion as a means to power.

Pentecostalism and the Rise of Political Christianity

The emergence of Christian revivalism and Pentecostalism in Nigeria is closely associated with the historic rivalries over national power and resources, particularly between Christians and Muslims, alluded to above. Adogame terms this trend a "Christian scramble for a role in national public life" (2005:130), in a state perceived to be successively governed and dominated by a Muslim governing class. Until the 1990s, Nigerian Christians were largely politically docile. The umbrella Christian organisation, the Christian Association of Nigeria (CAN) – established in 1976 – initially adopted a conservative and passive stance in national politics.

This was eventually to become a proactive one in the wake of the growing Christian perception of the creeping islamisation of the Nigerian political space, particularly in the context of General Babangida's and later General Abacha's transition to civilian democracy and the religiously motivated violence characteristic of that period. In 1989, CAN issued a statement urging "genuine properly born-again Christians, filled with the Holy Spirit" to "come and contest elections" under the military's transition to civil rule programme (CAN, 1989, cited in Obadare, 2006:668). CAN further argued that "Christians ought to be interested in politics, which is the vehicle used in reaching the position of leadership in this country" (*ibid.*). With the establishment of the Pentecostal Fellowship of Nigeria (PFN) in 1991, the stage was set for renewed and determined Christian activism. During this phase, Pentecostalists became very outspoken about marginalisation and the ill-treatment of Christians, and also sought power through electoral contests to "make change happen". Thus, for instance, S.T.

Akande, the general secretary of the Nigerian Baptist Mission, eventually joined the race in the presidential primaries.

It is worth noting that throughout Nigeria's postcolonial history, the tides of Pentecostalism and Christian revivalism have often been strengthened by specific national political events and factors – for instance, the adoption of Shari'a by some Northern states since 1999 and the admonition by two former "Muslim" presidents (General Buhari and Shehu Shagari) that Muslims not vote for non-Muslims. Presently, Pentecostalism has become an entrenched part of Nigeria's social and political landscape. Obasanjo only tapped into this bourgeoning religio-political movement by using his personal and political circumstances to identify with, and garner support from the Pentecostal community.

Initially jailed by General Abacha for his anti-regime stance, Obasanjo became born-again following his encounters with Pentecostal pastors who visited and prayed for his safe release from military incarceration in Yola Prison. On his release by General Abubakar following General Abacha's demise, Obasanjo became an active adherent of this "new Christianity". For its part, the Pentecostal movement saw Obasanjo as a messiah sent by God to liberate Nigerians and cleanse Nigeria of its dirty politics.

In the 1999 elections, Pentecostal Christians openly supported Obasanjo's candidature under the banner of the People's Democratic Party (PDP), viewing him as a symbol of the restoration of Christian control over the government of Nigeria and of the "ending of Muslim political dominance" (Ojo 2004:2). After Obasanjo was elected president, Pentecostal leaders conducted an all-night prayer meeting for him (Ojo 2004:2, 9). This gesture was politically endorsed and rewarded with the construction of a Pentecostal chapel in the presidential villa, the seat of national politics. As Obadare notes, Obasanjo's "victory at the polls and his eventual swearing-in as president on 29th May 1999 was heavily steeped in Christian Pentecostal symbolism" (2006:669), a drama that was spectacularly replayed in subsequent elections.

> To many Christians, Obasanjo's "second coming" was a spiritual metaphor, one that went beyond the ordinary fact of his fortuitous emergence as a beneficiary of political compromise between the country's geo-political power blocs … For Christians it was a fulfilment of God's promise to liberate his children (Southern Christians) from the yoke of northern (Muslim) leadership. A political exigent "second coming" was therefore invested with a spiritual halo, and Obasanjo himself became transformed into a virtual 'Messiah' almost overnight. (Obadare, 2006:669; our emphasis)

Conclusion

In this paper, we argue that religion, secularism and politics are embedded in the dialectics of Nigeria's heterogeneity, nation-state formation and cut-throat politics. Appeals to religious identities and profane imaginations are a commonplace in the armoury of politics and as a means to achieving power. It appears that Nigeria's political class – including the theocratic class or religious aristocracy – employ religious discourses and dogmas often to its advantage to mobilise and divide the people, and legitimise its hegemony over society.

Thus, the use and abuse of religion and politics is contingent on the stakes for power and egocentric orientation of stakeholders. Similarly, whilst confronting repression and abuse of power – particularly in dire circumstances –, the elite of Nigeria's organised religions have, in the main, aligned themselves with the political class in perpetuating elite hegemony. We also argue that religions have the capacity to generate a "theocratic class", for instance in Obasanjo's Pentecostal constituency and as political allies of the Northern Islamic fundamentalist and other pro-Shari'a elements, whose support for governors was contingent on the adoption of the Shari'a.

Furthermore, in the context of Shari'a in the North, we have seen the emergence of political Islam, arguably as a political force used by elements seeking to undermine Obasanjo's national power and influence by ostensibly exploiting loopholes within the so-called "secular" state – e.g., certain provisions in the 1999 Constitution relating to freedom of religion and concurrent legislation.

The religious factor is deeply embedded in Nigerian politics, and it is very difficult to see how its influence can be overcome. This study confirms the following powerful claim:

> *Nigeria has witnessed a surge in the phenomenon of Christian and Islamic religious fundamentalism or revivalism. Rather than Secularisation, there is a puritanical tendency emerging in religious practice and this tendency is producing new political actors. (International IDEA, 2000:74)*

Given the pervasiveness of religion in politics, the best option is to accept religion as a social reality and to take creative measures to reverse its adverse and intrusive effects, particularly in relation to politics and democratic governance. Such measures should target the disengagement of religion from politics in a multiethnic society such as Nigeria, link up citizenship rights with the deepening of democracy, promote grassroots inter-faith post-conflict reconciliation, and include public enlightenment programmes designed to reduce tensions between both dominant religions in Nigeria. What is required is a thorough process of social transformation and the genuine entrenchment and institutionalisation of multicultural and non-sectarian narratives in the hearts and minds of political stakeholders, both constitutionally and in terms of actual practice.

Acknowledgement
We are indebted to Nordic Africa Institute's two anonymous reviewers for making critical comments and suggestions on the initial draft of this paper.

Bibliography

Adogame, Afe (2006) "Politicization of religion and religionization of politics in Nigeria" in Korieh, C.J. and Nwokeji, G.U. (eds), *Religion, History, and Politics in Nigeria*. Oxford: University Press of America.

Agbaje, Adigun, Rashidi Okunola and Wale Adebanwi (2005) *Religious pluralism and democratic governance in South-Western Nigeria*. Research Report submitted to Centre for Research and Documentation, Kano.

ASC (Africa Studies Centre, Leiden University) (2008) *Web Resources on Nigeria and Islam*, available: http://www.ascleiden.nl/Library/Webdossiers/NigeriaAndIslam.aspx, accessed: 07/08/2009

BBC (2002) *Talking Point*, 18 February 2002, 16:54 GMT, available on www.bbc.co.uk: accessed: 1/1/2008).

Binder, Leonard (1981) "Review of *Islam and Capitalism* by Maxime Rodinson, Brian Pearce", *American Journal of Sociology* 87, 2.

Beckman, Björn (1982) "Whose State? State and capitalist development in Nigeria", *Review of African Political Economy,* 23.

— (1981) "Imperialism and the national bourgeoisie", *Review of African Political Economy* 22.

Bosedau, Matthias and Alexander de Juan (March 2008) *The "Ambivalence of the Sacred in Africa": The Impact of Religion on Peace and Conflict in Africa,* GIGA WP 70/2008, German Institute of Global and Area Studies, available: http://www.giga-hamburg. de/dl/download.php?d=/content/publikationen/pdf/wp70_basedau-juan.pdf (accessed 28/08/2009).

Bujra, J. (2006) "Leo Igwe: Interview with a Nigerian Humanist", *Review of African Political Economy,* 33, 110.

Chubin, Shahram (1995) "The south and the new world order", in Brad Roberts (ed.), *Weapons Proliferations in the 1990s.* Cambridge/London: MIT Press.

Connolly, William (2000) *Why I am Not a Secularist.* Minneapolis: University of Minnesota Press.

Daily Trust (3 June 2003), Abuja: Trust Publications.

Falola, T. (1998) *Violence in Nigeria: The Crisis of Religious Politics and Secular Ideologies.* Rochester: University of Rochester Press.

Fanon, Frantz (1963) *Wretched of the Earth.* London: Macgibbon and Kee

FGN (Federal Republic of Nigeria) (1981) *Report of Tribunal of Inquiry on Kano Disturbances, (MAITATSINE).* Lagos: FGN

Francis, David (2006) (ed.), *Civil Militias: Africa's Intractable Security Menace?* Aldershot: Ashgate.

Global IDP (2003) *Training Workshop on the UN Guiding Principles on Internal Displacement.* Jos, Nigeria 17-19 February, www.idpproject.org/trainging.htm (accessed: 23/12/2006)

Greene, M. (2006) "Confronting categorical assumptions about the power of religion in Africa", *Review of African Political Economy* 33, 110.

Hanson, Stephanie (2007) "Nigeria's creaky political system". Council for Foreign Relations, available: http://www.cfr.org/publication/13079/nigerias_creaky_political_ system.html#7 (accessed: 06/12/2008).

Harneit-Sievers, A. (2007) "Bridging some of the gaps: inter-religious and inter-ethnic dialogues in Nigeria", BMZ-Federal Ministry for Economic Cooperation and Development (ed.), *Transforming Fragile States – Examples of Practical Experience* Germany. NOMOS and Federal Ministry of Economic Cooperation and Development.

Haynes, J. (2004) "Religion and democratization in Africa", *Democratization* 11, 4.

— (1997) *Democracy and Civil Society in the Third World: Politics and New Political Movements.* Malden MA: Blackwell.

— (1996) *Religion and Politics in Africa.* London: Zed Books.

Hoogvelt, Ankie (1979) "Indigenisation and foreign capital: industrialisation in Nigeria", *Review of African Political Economy,* 14.

Huntington, S.P. (1993) "The clash of civilizations?' *Foreign Affairs* 72, 3.

— (1997) *The Clash of Civilizations and the Remaking of a New World Order.* New York: Simon and Schuster.

Ilo, Stan Chu (15 March 2009) "Pope's visit to Africa: Matters arising", *Nigeria World,* available: http://nigeriaworld.com/articles/2009/mar/152.html (accessed: 01/09/2009)

International IDEA (Institute for Democracy and Electoral Assistance) (2001) *Democracy in Nigeria: Continuing Dialogue for Nation-Building.* Lagos: International IDEA.

Kenny, J. (1996) "Shari'a and Christianity in Nigeria: Islam and a 'secular' state", *Journal of Religion in Africa.* 26, 4.

— (1986) "Shari'a in Nigeria: a historical survey", *Bulletin on Islam and Christian-Muslim Relations in Africa* 4, 1.

Kukah, M.H. (1993) *Religion, Politics and Power in Northern Nigeria.* Ibadan: Spectrum Books

Lubeck, P.M. (1985) "Islamic protest under semi-industrial capitalism: 'Yan Tatsine explained', *Africa* (Special Issue on *Popular Islam)* 55, 4.

Love, Roy (2006) "Religion, ideology and conflict in Africa", *Review of African Political Economy* 33, 110.

Mamdani, M. (2005) *Good Muslim, Bad Muslim: America, the Cold War and the Roots of Terror.* New York: Three Leaves Press.

Mazrui, Ali (1986) "A trinity of cultures in Nigerian politics: The religious Impact", *Africa Events* 2, 10 (October).

Obadare, Ebenezer (2006) "Pentecostal presidency? The Lagos-Ibadan 'Theocratic Class' and the Muslim 'other'", *Review of African Political Economy* 33, 110.

Odion-Ahkaine, Sylvester (2006) "Liberation theology in Nigeria?" *Review of African Political Economy* 33, 110.

Ojo, M.A. (2004) "Pentecostalism, public accountability and governance in Nigeria". Paper presented at the workshop on Pentecostal-Civil Society Dialogue on Public Accountability and Governance, Lagos, 18 October.

Omeje, Kenneth (2007) "Oil conflict and accumulation politics in Nigeria". *Environmental Change and Security Project Report No. 12, 2006/7.* Washington DC: Woodrow Wilson International Centre for Scholars.

— (2006) "The Egbesu and Bakassi Boys: African spiritism and mystical re-traditionalisation of religion", in D.J. Francis (ed.), *Civil Militias: Africa's Intractable Security Menace?* Aldershot: Ashgate.

Onaiyekan, John (1987) "The Shariah in Nigeria: a Christian view", *Bulletin on Islam and Christian-Muslim Relations in Africa* 5, 3.

Paden, J.N. (2005) *Muslim Civic Cultures and Conflict Resolution: The Challenge of Democratic Federalism in Nigeria.* Washington: Brookings Institution Press.

Robinson, M. (1978) *Islam and Capitalism* (trans. Brian Pearce). Austin: University of Texas Press.

Ruby, Roberts and Samuel Shah (22 March 2007) "Nigeria's presidential elections: the Christian-Muslim divide", Pew Research Centre Publications, available: http://pewresearch.org/pubs/435/nigeria-presidential-election (accessed: 06/08/2009)

Shettima, A.G. (2004) *The Anambra Ritual Killings: Matters Arising;* available: www.amanaonline.com (accessed: 13/07/2009).

Sulaiman, I. (1987) "Which Constitution?" *Africa Events* 3, 12 (December): 29-42.

Tar, U.A. (2009) *The Politics of Neoliberal Democracy in Africa: State and Civil Society in Nigeria.* London/New York: I.B. Tauris.

— (2007) "A hollow giant on agile feet? The challenges of democratic consolidation in Nigeria", *African Renaissance.* 4, 3 and 4.

— and Alfred Zack-Williams (2007) "Nigeria: contested elections and an unstable democracy', *Review of African Political Econom*y 113.

Tell Magazine, No. 46, 15 November 1999 (Lagos).

The Economist (2007) "The World in 2008".

The NEWS, Vol.19, No.24, 16 December 2002 (Lagos).

This Day, Sunday, 8 August 2004 (Lagos).

Tilly, C. (1975) "Reflections on the history of European state-making', in Tilly, C. (ed.), *The Formation of National States in Western Europe.* Princeton: University Press.

Usman, Y.B., and A. Abba (2000) *The Misrepresentation of Nigeria: The Facts and the Figures.* Zaria: Centre for Democratic Research and Training (CEDDERT).

Williams, G. (1980) *State and Society in Nigeria.* Idanre: Afrografika Publishers.

Yared, N.S. (2002) *Secularism and the Arab World, 1850-1939.* London: Saqi Books.

Zagorin, Perez (2003) *How the Idea of Religious Toleration Came to the West.* Princeton: Princeton University Press.

DISCUSSION PAPERS PUBLISHED BY THE INSTITUTE

Recent issues in the series are available electronically for download free of charge
www.nai.uu.se

1. Kenneth Hermele and Bertil Odén, *Sanctions and Dilemmas. Some Implications of Economic Sanctions against South Africa.* 1988. 43 pp. ISBN 91-7106-286-6

2. Elling Njål Tjönneland, *Pax Pretoriana. The Fall of Apartheid and the Politics of Regional Destabilisation.* 1989. 31 pp. ISBN 91-7106-292-0

3. Hans Gustafsson, Bertil Odén and Andreas Tegen, *South African Minerals. An Analysis of Western Dependence.* 1990. 47 pp. ISBN 91-7106-307-2

4. Bertil Egerö, *South African Bantustans. From Dumping Grounds to Battlefronts.* 1991. 46 pp. ISBN 91-7106-315-3

5. Carlos Lopes, *Enough is Enough! For an Alternative Diagnosis of the African Crisis.* 1994. 38 pp. ISBN 91-7106-347-1

6. Annika Dahlberg, *Contesting Views and Changing Paradigms.* 1994. 59 pp. ISBN 91-7106-357-9

7. Bertil Odén, *Southern African Futures. Critical Factors for Regional Development in Southern Africa.* 1996. 35 pp. ISBN 91-7106-392-7

8. Colin Leys and Mahmood Mamdani, *Crisis and Reconstruction – African Perspectives.* 1997. 26 pp. ISBN 91-7106-417-6

9. Gudrun Dahl, *Responsibility and Partnership in Swedish Aid Discourse.* 2001. 30 pp. ISBN 91-7106-473-7

10. Henning Melber and Christopher Saunders, *Transition in Southern Africa – Comparative Aspects.* 2001. 28 pp. ISBN 91-7106-480-X

11. *Regionalism and Regional Integration in Africa.* 2001. 74 pp. ISBN 91-7106-484-2

12. Souleymane Bachir Diagne, et al., *Identity and Beyond: Rethinking Africanity.* 2001. 33 pp. ISBN 91-7106-487-7

13. Georges Nzongola-Ntalaja, et al., *Africa in the New Millennium.* Edited by Raymond Suttner. 2001. 53 pp. ISBN 91-7106-488-5

14. *Zimbabwe's Presidential Elections 2002.* Edited by Henning Melber. 2002. 88 pp. ISBN 91-7106-490-7

15. Birgit Brock-Utne, *Language, Education and Democracy in Africa.* 2002. 47 pp. ISBN 91-7106-491-5

16. Henning Melber et al., *The New Partnership for Africa's Development (NEPAD).* 2002. 36 pp. ISBN 91-7106-492-3

17. Juma Okuku, *Ethnicity, State Power and the Democratisation Process in Uganda.* 2002. 42 pp. ISBN 91-7106-493-1

18. Yul Derek Davids, et al., *Measuring Democracy and Human Rights in Southern Africa.* Compiled by Henning Melber. 2002. 50 pp. ISBN 91-7106-497-4

19. Michael Neocosmos, Raymond Suttner and Ian Taylor, *Political Cultures in Democratic South Africa.* Compiled by Henning Melber. 2002. 52 pp. ISBN 91-7106-498-2

20. Martin Legassick, *Armed Struggle and Democracy. The Case of South Africa.* 2002. 53 pp. ISBN 91-7106-504-0

21. Reinhart Kössler, Henning Melber and Per Strand, *Development from Below. A Namibian Case Study.* 2003. 32 pp. ISBN 91-7106-507-5

22. Fred Hendricks, *Fault-Lines in South African Democracy. Continuing Crises of Inequality and Injustice.* 2003. 32 pp. ISBN 91-7106-508-3

23. Kenneth Good, *Bushmen and Diamonds. (Un)Civil Society in Botswana.* 2003. 39 pp. ISBN 91-7106-520-2

24. Robert Kappel, Andreas Mehler, Henning Melber and Anders Danielson, *Structural Stability in an African Context.* 2003. 55 pp. ISBN 91-7106-521-0

25. Patrick Bond, *South Africa and Global Apartheid. Continental and International Policies and Politics.* 2004. 45 pp. ISBN 91-7106-523-7

26. Bonnie Campbell (ed.), *Regulating Mining in Africa. For whose benefit?* 2004. 89 pp. ISBN 91-7106-527-X

27. Suzanne Dansereau and Mario Zamponi, *Zimbabwe – The Political Economy of Decline.* Compiled by Henning Melber. 2005. 43 pp. ISBN 91-7106-541-5

28. Lars Buur and Helene Maria Kyed, *State Recognition of Traditional Authority in Mozambique. The Nexus of Community Representation and State Assistance.* 2005. 30 pp. ISBN 91-7106-547-4

29. Hans Eriksson and Björn Hagströmer, *Chad – Towards Democratisation or Petro-Dictatorship?* 2005. 82 pp. ISBN 91-7106-549-0

30. Mai Palmberg and Ranka Primorac (eds), *Skinning the Skunk – Facing Zimbabwean Futures.* 2005. 40 pp. ISBN 91-7106-552-0

31. Michael Brüntrup, Henning Melber and Ian Taylor, *Africa, Regional Cooperation and the World Market – Socio-Economic Strategies in Times of Global Trade Regimes.* Compiled by Henning Melber. 2006. 70 pp. ISBN 91-7106-559-8

32. Fibian Kavulani Lukalo, *Extended Handshake or Wrestling Match? – Youth and Urban Culture Celebrating Politics in Kenya.* 2006. 58 pp. ISBN 91-7106-567-9

33. Tekeste Negash, *Education in Ethiopia: From Crisis to the Brink of Collapse.* 2006. 55 pp. ISBN 91-7106-576-8

34. Fredrik Söderbaum and Ian Taylor (eds), *Micro-Regionalism in West Africa. Evidence from Two Case Studies.* 2006. 32 pp. ISBN 91-7106-584-9

35. Henning Melber (ed.), *On Africa – Scholars and African Studies.* 2006. 68 pp. ISBN 978-91-7106-585-8

36. Amadu Sesay, *Does One Size Fit All? The Sierra Leone Truth and Reconciliation Commission Revisited.* 2007. 56 pp. ISBN 978-91-7106-586-5

37. Karolina Hulterström, Amin Y. Kamete and Henning Melber, *Political Opposition in Africn Countries – The Case of Kenya, Namibia, Zambia and Zimbabwe.* 2007. 86 pp. ISBN 978-7106-587-2

38. Henning Melber (ed.), *Governance and State Delivery in Southern Africa. Examples from Botswana, Namibia and Zimbabwe.* 2007. 65 pp. ISBN 978-91-7106-587-2

39. Cyril Obi (ed.), *Perspectives on Côte d'Ivoire: Between Political Breakdown and Post-Conflict Peace.* 2007. 66 pp. ISBN 978-91-7106-606-6

40. Anna Chitando, *Imagining a Peaceful Society. A Vision of Children's Literature in a Post-Conflict Zimbabwe.* 2008. 26 pp. ISBN 978-91-7106-623-7

41. Olawale Ismail, *The Dynamics of Post-Conflict Reconstruction and Peace Building in West Africa. Between Change and Stability.* 2009. 52 pp. ISBN 978-91-7106-637-4

42. Ron Sandrey and Hannah Edinger, *Examining the South Africa–China Agricultural Trading Relationship.* 2009. 58 pp. ISBN 978-91-7106-643-5

43. Xuan Gao, *The Proliferation of Anti-Dumping and Poor Governance in Emerging Economies.* 2009. 41 pp. ISBN 978-91-7106-644-2

44. Lawal Mohammed Marafa, *Africa's Business and Development Relationship with China. Seeking Moral and Capital Values of the Last Economic Frontier.* 2009. 21 pp. ISBN 978-91-7106-645-9

45. Mwangi wa Githinji, *Is That a Dragon or an Elephant on Your Ladder? The Potential Impact of China and India on Export Led Growth in African Countries.* 2009. 40 pp. ISBN 978-91-7106-646-6

46. Jo-Ansie van Wyk, *Cadres, Capitalists, Elites and Coalitions. The ANC, Business and Development in South Africa.* 2009. 61 pp. ISBN 978-91-7106-656-5

47. Elias Courson, *Movement for the Emancipation of the Niger Delta (MEND). Political Marginalization, Repression and Petro-Insurgency in the Niger Delta.* 2009. 30 pp. ISBN 978-91-7106-657-2

48. Babatunde A. Ahonsi, *Gender Violence and HIV/AIDS in Post-Conflict West Africa.* 2010, 38 pp. ISBN 978-91-7106- 665-7

49. Usman Tar and Abba Gana Shettima, *Endangered Democracy? The Struggle over Secularism and its Implications for Politics and Democracy in Nigeria.* 2010, 21 pp. ISBN 978-91-7106-666-4

www.ingramcontent.com/pod-product-compliance
Lightning Source LLC
Chambersburg PA
CBHW080210300326
41934CB00039B/3449